Please God…

34 Days to Radical Self Respect

How To Be More Assertive

Adult Coloring Book

34 Days of Ways to Celebrate You, Walk Away
or Say No When You Must

Without Annoying Anyone, Including You

Aunti Says

Published by ProRisk Press

Box 253, Alberta Beach, Alberta Canada T0E 0A0

Patricia@auntisays.com

Patriciaogilvie.com

Copyright © 2016 Aunti Says

Cover Design © 2016 Cover Designed by Prorisk Press

Stock images from GraphicStock

All rights reserved. No part of this publication may be reproduced or transmitted in any form or by any means, including informational storage and retrieval systems, without permission in writing from the copyright holder, except for brief quotations in a review.

ISBN 978-0-9780520-6-5

Modern First Edition Series Printing 2016

"You cannot live a brave life without disappointing some people. Don't let it be yourself" – AuntiSays

If you like this little purse sized adult coloring book, you'll love the 1st and 2nd Adult Coloring Books in this Series of stress reducers and fun increasers.

Look here for Bag Lady and Marbles

Www.auntisays.com/shop/

Day 1. An assertive woman will….

…. automatically stop trying to please when she feels unwanted or unappreciated. She won't fix it or beg, she'll simply walk away. Today, if you need to, walk away.

Color the letters of inspiration and then color the corresponding picture like the example here.

34 Days to Radical Self Respect

Praise for *34 Days to Radical Self Respect... How To Be More Assertive*

"Congratulations to an awesome person who had a vision and went on to be a super star. This is amazing!

– Christine Nichiporik

"What a delightful, creative and fun way to face color-through fears. We can all benefit from Aunti Says."

- Patricia Morgan

"A whimsical and poignant approach to the deeply held fear of not having enough... In this delightful coloring book for adults, Aunti Says names the elephant that invades so many of our living rooms. With a combination of practical wisdom, and creative expression, she engages the strength of our hearts, as well as our understanding, to help us create lives rich in all we need and love. I highly recommend it!"

- Elizabeth Love

"Without a doubt, taking a page a day has improved my attitude about money, debt and confidence I deserve a quality lifestyle. Reducing anxiety is the key."

- Pearl Buck

Dedication

This extraordinary coloring book is inspired by and dedicated to all the women in my life who needed a push and pull to put themselves first… however infrequently. Finding ways to take better care of themselves and to honor the self is one of the greatest gifts one can give oneself. It's your turn to be a strong woman. Love you all.

Acknowledgements

To my sisters in life and biggest supporters enabling me to live a healthy lifestyle and honoring one another.

To my teachers and examples throughout life, who have been an integral part of my growing and learning to love myself. I love and appreciate you all.

And to my family who always have tricks up their sleeves how to enjoy life.

Aunty Says

Introduction

"34 Days of Radical Self Respect . . . Be More Assertive" can be taken with you anywhere; add a smile, a pack of cultured pens, pencils or crayons and allow it to take you through a proven process to tap into how to reduce the fears of losing yourself in and amongst all the noise in the world.

Listen, you can't change how other people feel, ever. You can only change how you feel about yourself, what you do and what you don't do.

What this also means to me is that if those people who scoff, judge and get disappointed with what you do or don't do, they don't have your back in the first place. That's okay. People who care for you and want to see you excel, will not be disappointed. They are your cheerleaders.

They stand by you.

They are your life supporters, even if you don't need them all the time.

People who are disappointed have their own agenda. Their agenda is not aligned with yours, it doesn't matter, does it?

What does this have to do with being more assertive and stronger? When you surround yourself with the people who are rooting for your rise, it's going to be okay and as a result, know in your heart and mind; you are strong to move forward.

All it takes is learning a few basic skills how to say no, how to set boundaries, how to listen to your intuition, and eventually you won't even need one other person to stand by you. You will remind yourself that you are brave and strong. That's what keeps you moving forward. Sometimes it's just you.

If at times, you feel all alone, here's what you do.

Grab a pencil crayon or fine marker.

Any colors you want - in fact, grab a handful.

There is room in the margins of these pages for writing in your C.R.A.P. about justifying why everyone else should be first in line and you last.

It's time to celebrate who you are and increase you own Zen energy while changing your mental state from focusing on them to finally focusing on you.

It's time to be brave and strong for yourself, especially if you need to walk away or say no.

It's okay.

Applying the latest trending books is visionary. Applying trending adult coloring books for a specific issue like fear of self-worth, self love, safety or trusting and putting your whole self in front of you is poignant and you should be proud that you are willing to take whatever it takes to love yourself.

I promise if you bring these 34 simple ways into your life, offering a vision and simple plan of action to reduce normal stress, especially over holidays, you will be surprised and pleased at the results. You will discover some unique and known ways to assert yourself.

What a great idea – your mental health solution to stay strong, even in the face of adversity. Others should be put ahead of you? Bull droppings!

You are probably the kind of person who sees opportunities and one of a kind special soul your family and friends marvel at. I bet you take action immediately.

The concept of coloring to reduce stress and increase self-awareness is a big-ticket item in today's fast paced hectic world. And you're about to experience a powerful little book to keep your sanity while valuing yourself more. It's time you celebrated you.

This book will guide you page by page to train yourself to focus on positive thoughts long enough for them to manifest and produce more positive thoughts. You will begin to feel better about celebrating who you are. You begin to be a strong woman. Because, when you celebrate you, others will automatically pick up on that energy and celebrate you too.

The contrary, you know well enough, is you could get taken advantage of. It's now time to stop that.

It's now time to be more assertive and celebrate you.

The rules are simple: 1. Smile 2. Grab a crayon 3. Trace the words of inspiration on each page 4. Color the mandalas and pictures. Aunti has your back and stands by you.

Aunti Says

The airplane, the atomic bomb, and the zipper have cured me of any tendency to state that a thing can't be done. - R.I. Duffus

Now your turn:

Day 2. Snack On An Orange

Your co-workers will think you're just craving a juicy mid-day snack, but besides satisfying tummy grumbles, you'll be reaping the benefits of the stress-relieving powers of citrus. Research shows that a dose of vitamin C helps people bounce back more easily from a stressful situation. Celebrate by reducing stress. Today, eat an orange (and everyday)

"What each of us believes in, is up to us, but life is impossible without believing in something."

— Kentetsu Takamori

Day 3. All the more reason to believe in yourself. To use the power of believing in yourself to your greatest benefit, you first need to become self-aware. Then you can attune your beliefs to your deepest spiritual aspirations. Tell yourself today day, "I love you."

Truth is, a belief is just your perspective on something. Some work, some don't. Practice saying "I love you." (And everyday)

"I am good, but not an angel. I do sin, but I am not the devil. I am just a small girl in a big world trying to find someone to love."

— Marilyn Monroe

Day 4. Ah dear Marilyn. If you only knew that the first one to love is yourself. Today, write yourself a love note, carry it with you all the time and pull it out frequently to remind and celebrate who you are - a loving and caring person.

34 Days to Radical Self Respect

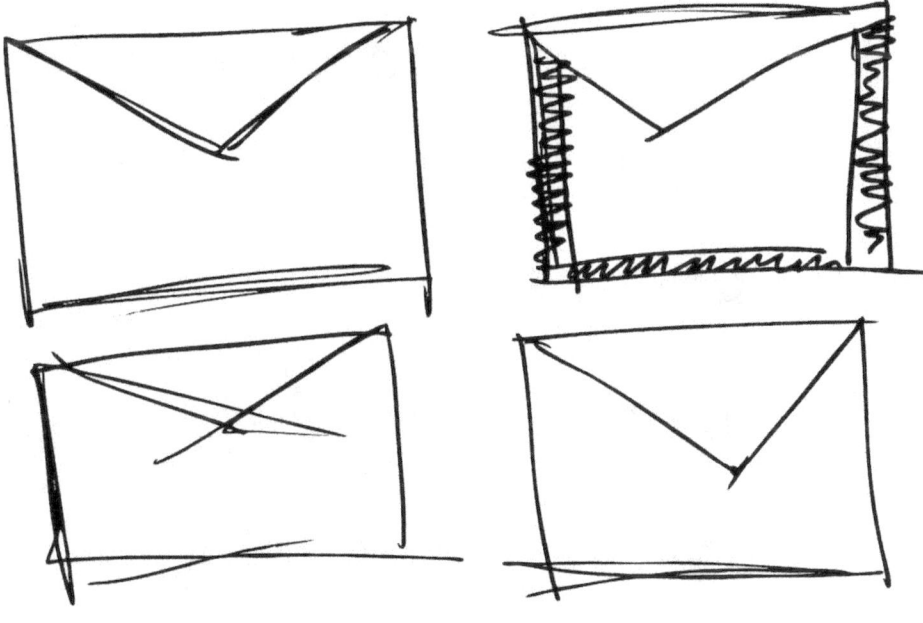

Day 5. The injunction that we should love our neighbors as ourselves means to us equally that we should love ourselves as we love our neighbors."

— Barbara Deming

Today, find one thing to love about yourself. (And everyday)

Day 6. The best celebration of self is to take time to be quiet enough to hear the genuine within yourself so you can hear it in others.

Do yoga by yourself or meditate at least 15 minutes today to still the chatter in your brain and hear the voice of your true self. (And everyday)

Day 7: I love a party. Don't you? Go dancing and meet some new people. Or just take one of your good friends and go for a walk or sit for a cup of tea.

(Or sip a glass of wine...)

Either way, moving with a friend is very important to keep yourself focused on how much you mean to you.

Trust yourself to make the right decision for you.

Day 8: The next most important thing to believe about yourself is that no matter what age you are, or what your circumstances might be, you are special, and you still have something unique to offer. Your life, because of who you are, has meaning. Know this inside out.

Today look yourself in the mirror and smile. Tell yourself you are special.

34 Days to Radical Self Respect

Day 9: Focus on one task at a time. Remember, it's your place in the world; it's your life. Go on and do all you can with it, and make it the life you want to live. This way you are honoring that you are safe and trusting. You are celebrating who you are.

Day 10: Frequently visualize and affirm success in your chosen profession. Your visions and words play a large role in determining the outcome of your desires.

Remember: Joy attracts perfect people - worry repels perfect people. Give any anxiety to God through prayer, and put your whole focus upon "How may I serve?" Trust that as you give, the universe gives back.

Day 11: Treat yourself to something special. How about some new lingerie?

Something sexy and new always brings out the vamp in you.

34 Days to Radical Self Respect

Day 12: Spend an afternoon shopping for something special. Even if you don't have the money, go window shopping and pretend you are treating yourself. Pretend you have $100 in your pocket and when you see something, tell yourself, I could buy that. I could buy that. You may spend that $100, 20 times in a day. Your subconscious loves you.

Day 13. Visit your local pet shop and enjoy the yipping yapping and meowing of the cute animals. Better yet, play with your favorite pet.

Stay in the moment - this way you celebrate you and the pet celebrates you too.

Day 14. What's your favorite flower? Buy yourself a single stem every week to show your appreciation and celebration of you.

Smell it, admire it, love it because it's your gift to yourself.

Day 15. Snap a photo of something that puts a smile on your. A sunset, a sunrise, the moon, a flower, a bird. Family. Visit the zoo and see something unusual.

What brings you joy, is what your true self needs right now.

Develop that photo. Put in a frame or on your smart phone for you to see each day. Allow that smile.

Day 16. Color

Color like you did as a child.

Color inside the lines or outside - doesn't matter.

Bring your child out and enjoy at least 5 minutes each day coloring.

That's why you have this book. Enjoy.

Day 17. Today change your mind about exercise. Call it "activity" not "exercise" and remind yourself that your body needs to move.

Honor it. Celebrate it with a walk, a climb, and complain a little less.

Choose activities that you love. Every day.

Day 18. I have learned over the years that any happiness I get, I've got to make myself. And the first step is to reduce stress in my life.

Over time, stress causes vascular changes and chemical imbalances that damage my brain and other cells in my body.

Find what causes you the most stress. Acknowledge it. Thank it. Then move it out with activity.

Day 19. Ask for help. Pray to spirit, your God, the angels who watch over you, your family, friends, even a stranger.

You deserve to ask for what you want. Help isn't a reward; it's an effect.

It's the effect of taking more conscious care of yourself. ASK.

Day 20. Sift through your social media. Clear out those who are negative and caustic to your better nature.

Take assertive action and find better friends!

Hey, I shouldn't laugh, but if my friends are bullies and talking negative, I need to make a change.

Today do what feels in your heart to be right for you - you may be criticized anyway. Damned if you do and damned if you don't. Take care of you.

Day 21. Today practice giving and receiving at least three times. When someone offers to help you, smile and say, "Yes, please" or "Thank you."

Give any guilt or other harsh emotions to God and the angels. If you get a strong gut feeling not to interact with someone, follow your gut.

Day 22. Know in your bones, head and heart what you want and say it out loud, write it down, share it in confidence. Then take the first step. Any action you take will open doors for you.

So do something today and every single day related to your dream.

Day 23. Take a REAL day off to play in the city. Practice being in the moment and mindful. Awaken your senses to the shapes and sizes around you. Steel, concrete, a tree, a flower, more iron.

Never hurry. This time NO shopping, just looking and smelling and breathing in.

Possess your time. Walk and look around you.

Day 24. Look, you have to reduce stress before you can move in any direction.

How did it get this way? Stress is a bugger that needs to be dealt with.

Get out in nature. Make a date with the Mother of All Earth. You visited the city. Now it's time to go nature sightseeing. Do a country field day and let the sounds and smells lure you into relaxation.

Day 25. Ask yourself," How much resistance are you in, now, to learning more about yourself?" Put your hand on your heart, and ask, "How much am I vested in staying the same because I want to be right about how life works in my world?"

Imagine a gauge with a dial. Reach out and turn the dial down a bit. You will feel better even if it's just a small notch. That's it; dial it down until you can feel yourself freeing resistance to learning more.

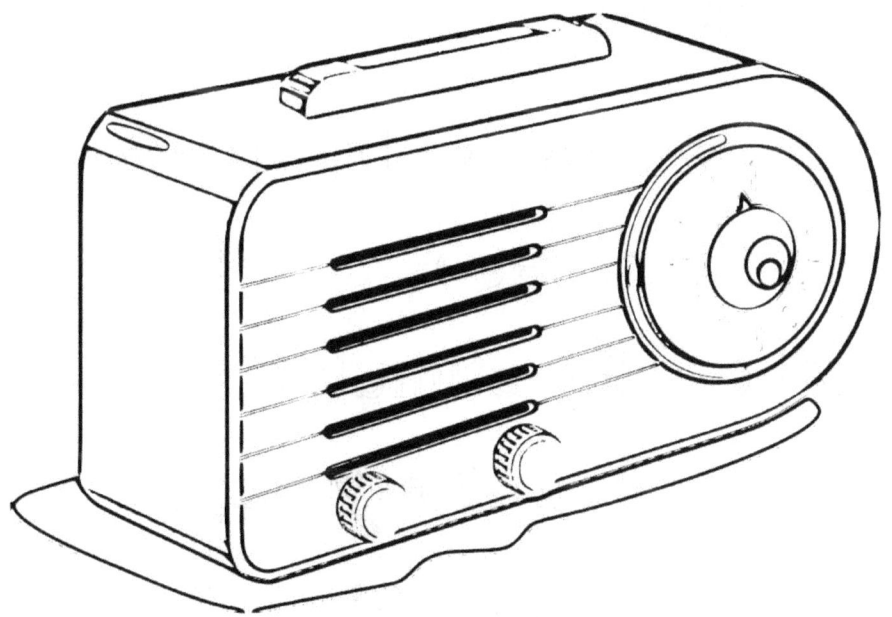

Day 26. What excites your inner kid and artistic mood? Adult coloring books!

Reduces brain fatigue and increases good mood. By stimulating your mind every day, your can preserve your memory and your sanity. Grab those crayons and start coloring!

Day 27. List old fears and beliefs - you know those voices in your head. Examine this list and decide if any are true for you right now.

Replace any of these with positive statements or affirmations. If you've been repeating "I'm a failure at everything!" replace it with "I am successful in these areas in my life (fill in the blank)."

With each item, ask yourself how true are they right now. It's time to decide once and for all if it is serving you or hindering you.

Day 28. New habits can include:

- Restrict TV, telephone, video, web, social media time and use them as rewards only.
- Write, read, sew, study, or whatever that requires your attention for completion, in a quiet area free of distractions.
- Put up a "Do Not Disturb" sign to show your kids, spouse and friends you value your time.
- Restructure your time with work and play to gain the most time advantages to complete projects.
- Get an accountability partner – someone who will support you.

Day 29. Hobbies are good for you because they allow you to LOVE the world; your soul knows better than best.

Let your artful and childlike spirit go on a generous adventure (Africa?) and
hobby - it - up!

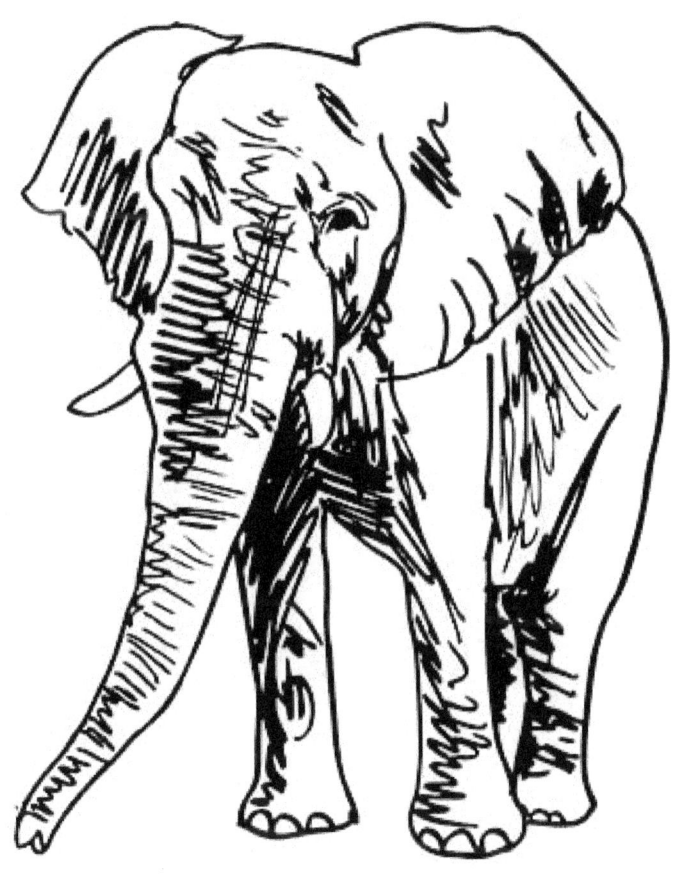

Day 30. Validate, validate, validate! If you don't experience authentic validation for who you are and what you offer, no one else will either. Today, acknowledge yourself for absolutely everything you've done and for absolutely everything you haven't done. That's right, for everything today. Practice validating yourself every day.

Day 31. Pick one day a week when you could spend completely for yourself.

Challenge yourself to become aware of your thoughts and words.

Catch yourself complaining and stop it. Continue to validate yourself at every chance you can. Notice how you feel at the end of the day. Write about it. Then go to sleep.

Day 32. When you get clarity about what is most important to you, you get vision.

Here are a few ways to develop vision.

- Be yourself -- trust yourself.
- Work and love strongly.
- Make your business such a safe place that you never experience failure or invalidation.
- If you make a mistake, try again.

Day 33. Know what you don't want.

But then, turn it around and know what you do want.

You will achieve it without invalidating who you are.

34 Days to Radical Self Respect

Day 34. Repeat Daily:

I create my Beliefs. My Beliefs determine what I do and how I feel. Therefore, I create my life and I can change it. I take my power back and mold my life my way!

(and so it is)

"When a woman becomes her own best friend life is easier." - Furstenberg

Thank You for Being Here!

If you like this little purse sized adult coloring book, you'll love the 1st and 2nd Adult Coloring Books in this series of stress reducers and fun increasers.

Look for more in the Series here:

Www.auntisays.com/shop/

Aunty Says

www.ingramcontent.com/pod-product-compliance
Lightning Source LLC
Chambersburg PA
CBHW061340040426
42444CB00011B/3008